BIG BUCK BU$INESS

SKIN DEEP
THE BUSINESS OF BEAUTY

by Angela Royston

Gareth Stevens
Publishing

Please visit our website, www.garethstevens.com. For a free color catalog of all our high-quality books, call toll free 1-800-542-2595 or fax 1-877-542-2596.

Library of Congress Cataloging-in-Publication Data

Royston, Angela, 1945-
Skin deep : the business of beauty / Angela Royston.
    p. cm. — (Big-buck business)
Includes index.
ISBN 978-1-4339-7764-0 (pbk.)
ISBN 978-1-4339-7765-7 (6-pack)
ISBN 978-1-4339-7763-3 (lib. bdg.)
1. Beauty culture. I. Title.
TT958.R695 2013
646.7'2—dc23

                    2012002830

First Edition

Published in 2013 by
Gareth Stevens Publishing
111 East 14th Street, Suite 349
New York, NY 10003

Produced by Calcium Creative Ltd
Designed by Nick Leggett
Edited by Sarah Eason and Vicky Egan
Picture research by Susannah Jayes

Photo credits: Cover: Shutterstock: Kayros Studio l, Aleksandr Markin r. Inside: Dreamstime: Goodscents 19br, Jperagine 31t; Istockphoto: Ariwasabi 3cr, Joel Carillet 11t, Diego Cervo 41t, Duncan1890 7, Ann Marie Kurtz 40bl, Catherine Lane 8cl, Kristian Sekulic 10cl; Shutterstock: Altafulla 5tc, Yuri Arcurs 43t, Anna Baburkina 35t, Dean Bertoncelj 29t, Diego Cervo 32tr, Claires 1br, Conrado 27t, Creatista 42b, Phil Date 38r, Dainis Derics 20b, Zhu Difeng 9t, Helga Esteb 36bl, 44bl, 45tr, SvetlanaFedoseyeva 18b, Richard Griffin 5br, Goodluz 21tr, CandyBox Images 33b, Raisa Kanareva 37tr, Yuganov Konstantin 24bl, Stuart Miles 15tr, Felix Mizioznikov 28cl, Luba V Nel 1bl, Vasilchenko Nikita 17r, Monika Olszewska 14–15c, Losevsky Pavel 13tr, Photobank.ch 12b, Andrey_Popov 23cl, Dooley Productions 26br, Gina Smith 16b, AISPIX by Image Source 30–31c, 34tr, 39c, SVLuma 13br, Szefei 22br, Liviu Toader 13bl, Vladimir Wrangel 6br, NataliaYeromina 4–5c, DUSAN ZIDAR 25tr.

Printed in the United States of America

CPSIA compliance information: Batch #CS12GS: For further information contact Gareth Stevens, New York, New York at 1-800-542-2595.

CONTENTS

FACING THE FUTURE

Do you see dollar signs when you look at your face? The cosmetic industry does! Every year, billions of dollars are spent on products that promise to make us look and feel great. So, who are the big beauty buyers of the future, and how is the industry cashing in on their obsession with good looks?

Forever young

In 2005, the average age girls began to use beauty products was 17. Today, it is just 13 years old, and girls as young as 6 are already wearing cosmetics! The industry hopes that by hooking these youthful cosmetic fans now, they will buy into beauty for the rest of their lives.

Every day, we are bombarded with images of gorgeous celebrities, models, and actresses. The pressure to look good has never been so intense!

4

Today, many men are choosing to have procedures such as Botox and other fillers to improve their looks.

Boys' beauty toys

These days, men aren't just splashing on aftershave. They are buying cleansers, exfoliators, and moisturizers, too! Today, men spend twice as much on beauty products as they did 10 years ago.

FUTURE FACT

Some $10.5 billion is spent on cosmetic procedures in the United States each year. If the industry keeps growing at its yearly rate of 5 percent, in 10 years time, it will take $17.1 billion of our money every year!

CHAPTER 1

A LONG HISTORY

SAFETY CONCERNS

As the beauty industry grew rapidly after 1950, people worried about how safe cosmetics were. In 1960, any color added to cosmetics in the United States had to be tested to make sure it did not cause cancer in people or animals. Other safety laws soon followed.

Is beauty a modern craze? Certainly more people are using more cosmetics today than ever before, but the idea of beauty is thousands of years old. Women in Ancient Egypt used black kohl to outline their eyes, and that was 6,000 years ago!

Rich and beautiful

In the past, cosmetics were used mainly by rich people and entertainers. In the 16th century, Queen Elizabeth I of England painted her face white to cover up smallpox scars and, as she got older, she dyed her hair red. In the 18th century, fashionable men and women powdered their faces and wore wigs.

This bust of Queen Nefertiti of Ancient Egypt shows her wearing kohl around her eyes.

6

Look like a movie star

Cosmetics became cheaper and more popular in the 1920s and 1930s. Women copied the look of Hollywood movie stars such as Greta Garbo. Max Factor supplied cosmetics for the stars of the screen and soon for ordinary people, too.

Queen Elizabeth I of England used cosmetics to make herself look younger and more beautiful.

How did the industry get to be so big? After World War II, the lives of people in the United States, Europe, and other richer countries changed dramatically. With peace came greater wealth and more spending money. Sales of refrigerators, televisions, and other home goods skyrocketed, and so did sales of cosmetics.

The giants

The United States leads the way in the cosmetics industry. Of the 100 biggest companies, nearly one-third are American, and their earnings have grown fast. For example, in 1983, Estée Lauder sold $1 billion worth of cosmetics. By 2009, just 26 years later, its sales had risen to $7.6 billion.

Estée Lauder products are some of the most widely sold cosmetics in the world.

ESTĒE LAUDER

BRONZE GODDESS
TINTED SELF-TAN
Golden Perfection
Tinted Self-Tanning Gelée for Body
Gel teinté auto-bronzant hâle parfait pour le corps

The demand for beauty products is rapidly growing in Asian countries.

Thousands of jobs

Many people are employed by the big beauty companies in research, factories, advertising, and sales. Many of the products created are bought by hairdressers, beauticians, manicurists, and other people with specialized skills. These people are employed in thousands of small businesses.

WHO'S BEHIND THE PRODUCT?

Where does the shampoo you use come from?

The simple answer is the store where you bought it, but a lot happens to shampoo and all beauty products before they reach the store. Beauty companies stay in business by producing a constant supply of new or improved products. In 2010, L'Oréal registered 612 new products!

Creating the product

Cosmetic chemists are scientists who experiment with ingredients and design new products. They find the best mixture of ingredients to give a particular result. The chemists then test the products to make sure they work and are safe.

A cosmetic chemist tests various chemicals to get the effect she wants, including the exact color and smell.

Many cosmetics companies choose celebrities, such as Eva Longoria, to promote their products.

Advertising and selling

Once the product is ready to launch, the advertising and sales departments go into action. They want customers to buy all their products, the existing ones as well as the new ones. Ads on billboards, television, and in magazines catch your eye, but sales people have to get the new products into stores and salons.

FUTURE FACT

Cosmetics companies advertise and sell their products online, as well as through the more usual outlets. In 2010, online sales were only 4 percent of the cosmetics industry's total sales, but this will almost certainly increase rapidly.

LOOKING GOOD

Who buys beauty products?

You might think the answer to that is "women," but men, too, want to look their best. Looking good makes people feel more confident. The beauty industry makes billions of dollars every year helping people to look as beautiful or handsome as possible.

Everyone wants to look their best when they are in a photo with their friends.

Many young men examine themselves in the mirror just as carefully as girls do.

Increasing demand

Cosmetics companies help to create the desire for beauty products. They encourage us to admire glamorous movie stars, models, and other celebrities, and want us to think that using the same cosmetics as the stars will make us more beautiful, too.

Billion-dollar businesses

Beauty companies such as L'Oréal sell billions of dollars' worth of cosmetics every year, and the amount is increasing. In 2008, L'Oréal sold $24 billion worth of cosmetics. By 2010, sales had increased to $27 billion.

WHAT THE WORLD SPENDS

In 2010, economists estimated that people spent $170 billion on cosmetics. About 27 percent was spent on skin care, 20 percent on hair care, 20 percent on makeup, and 33 percent on products such as sunscreens.

13

CHAPTER 2

MAKEUP MAGIC

What can makeup do for you? Makeup can subtly change the way your face looks. If your skin is too pale, blusher will add color. Makeup for eyes is designed to make eyes look bigger. Pale lipstick can make your lips look fuller, and bright lipstick can give you a dramatic look.

Variety of products

Each brand of cosmetics has a huge range of products, including dozens of colors of lipstick, eye shadow, and nail polish, as well as products for the skin. Each big company owns several different brands, so one company will produce and sell hundreds of different products.

Eye makeup includes eye shadow, eye liner, mascara, and eyebrow pencil.

FUTURE FACT

Men are beginning to buy makeup, such as concealer to cover zits and skin blemishes, and clear mascara for the eyelashes. The market is still small, but it is almost certain to become bigger in the future.

A mascara brush curls the eyelashes and applies mascara to make the eyelashes look thicker.

Selling technique

Companies that sell expensive brands, such as Estée Lauder, train their sales teams to also "link sell." A customer who goes into a store to buy lipstick, for example, will be encouraged to buy lip liner and lip gloss, too.

MAKEOVER

What's a makeover all about? A makeover is when a trained beautician selects products from a company's range and uses them to make up a customer. It benefits the customer and the cosmetic company. The customer has makeup applied by an expert, and the company sells lots of products.

FUTURE FACT

For decades, cosmetics were made for light-colored skin. It was not until the 1960s and 1970s that companies such as Flori Roberts and Astarté began to create products for African Americans. This is a fast-growing market around the world.

Helpful advice

There are so many makeup products to choose from, but many customers only buy their usual ones. In a makeover, the beautician will discuss all the products with the customer and choose the one that suits them best. This introduces the customer to new products.

Makeup for people of color is designed to compliment their skin tone.

Free samples

Giving away free samples is another way of tempting people to try the latest cosmetics. Once the customer has tried the sample, the company hopes that he or she will buy the product.

In some stores, a beautician will give a free makeover, but in most cases, the makeover has to be booked in advance and paid for.

17

LOOKING AFTER SKIN

How many different creams and lotions do you rub into your skin? The answer for most people is quite a few. Skin care is big business, partly because almost everyone uses skin-care products, including men, children, and even babies.

A baby's skin is soft and delicate. Special creams help stop it from drying out.

Clean and moist

From the moment you step under the shower, you are giving money to the cosmetics industry. You almost certainly use shower gel or soap, possibly followed by skin lotions of various types. Babies have their own range of products, from baby wipes to creams and oils. In spite of fewer babies being born, sales of baby care products in the United States increased by 2 percent in 2009.

Natural and organic

Sales of skin-care products that use natural ingredients are growing fast. In 2010, the sale of these cosmetics, including hair care and makeup, reached $7.7 billion. It is expected to increase to $11 billion or more by 2016.

Beauty companies are finding that products that carry a "no animal testing" label are selling well.

ANIMAL TESTING

Increasing sales of natural cosmetics may have been helped by groups who loudly oppose the practice of testing cosmetics on animals. These groups say that animal testing is not only cruel, but also unnecessary. Some countries in Europe now ban animal testing, but it continues in the United States.

NO ANIMAL TESTING

CRUELTY FREE

NO ANIMAL TESTING

DARKER OR LIGHTER?

What is the best color for skin?

There is, of course, no "best" color, but that doesn't stop people from spending money trying to make their skin darker or lighter. However, doctors warn that by doing so, many people are putting their health at risk.

Some people claim that using a tanning lamp or tanning bed is safer than sunbathing because you can control the amount of radiation that hits your skin.

Getting a tan

Many light-skinned people long to have a suntan. Sunscreens help to protect against the damaging effects of the sun's rays, but, amazingly, about half of all Americans never use sunscreen. Since the 1980s, tanning lamps and tanning beds have become much more popular, but both can cause skin cancer.

The sale of sun-care products is fairly constant, although it increases in particularly hot summers.

Lighten up

Skin lighteners are used to get rid of dark marks or acne scars, as well as to lighten skin tone. It is estimated that women in Asia spend $18 billion a year on skin lighteners. Many skin lighteners, however, contain bleach and other chemicals that can cause allergic rashes or skin cancer.

RED ALERT

Tanning beds are dangerous. The risk of someone who uses them getting skin cancer doubles after just seven sessions, and the younger the person is, the more dangerous it is. In 2012, California banned people younger than 18 years old from using tanning beds.

BEAUTY
TREATMENTS

A massage makes the skin healthy and glowing. It relaxes the muscles under the skin and so helps to soften frown lines.

Does a mud bath sound good to you? If so, a beauty treatment could be the thing for you! Beauty treatments can include facials, manicures for nails, and pedicures for feet. And that's only part of the deal. Customers can relax in steam rooms and pools, or indulge in aromatherapy or meditation.

Lie back and relax

The main purpose of going to a spa is to give your skin an intense workout, from deep cleaning to moisturizing. Exfoliation is a special type of scrub that gently rubs away the top layer of dead skin so that the creams can soak into the skin below.

Here comes the bride!

Spa days and facials are treats at any time, but they are especially popular before a wedding. The bride and bridesmaids may all buy the full treatment to make sure they look their best on the day of the wedding.

Painting toe nails is part of a pedicure.

FUTURE FACT

About 800,000 people worked in beauty salons and spas in 2008. By 2018, the US Department of Labor expects this will have increased by 20 percent. The number of skin-care specialists is expected to increase by almost 40 percent.

CHAPTER 3

ALL ABOUT HAIR

What is the easiest way to change the way you look? Changing your hairstyle is the most dramatic way to change your appearance. A different haircut can change the shape of your face. Changing the color of your hair and the amount of curl it has gives a whole new look.

The sale of shampoos dropped off during the economic recession that began in 2008. People bought fewer products and made sure they used every drop in the bottle.

Caring for hair

Hair care is big business. It includes shampoos, hair conditioners, mousses, and hairstyling products. In 2010, Americans spent $6.4 billion on hair care. The biggest companies include Estée Lauder, L'Oréal, and Proctor & Gamble. Each company makes a wide range of products that suit every type of hair.

Many men use hair gel to keep their hairstyle in place.

FUTURE FACT

Shampoos and conditioners that are made with organic ingredients cost more to buy, yet their sales are increasing faster than those of most beauty products. All the big companies have natural and organic brands, and some companies produce nothing else.

Growing hair care

Hair-care products have traditionally been aimed at women, but men are spending more and more money on hair care, too. Products that claim to reduce baldness are doing particularly well (see page 40).

25

HAIR
COLORANTS

Whatever the color...
Any natural hair color can be tinted or streaked with highlights. Techniques and coloring for dyeing hair are changing all the time. The color changes do not have to look natural. Bright pink, blue, and other colors are manufactured, too.

What are ombré and balayage? They are different ways of lightening your hair. The ombré look is having highlights that start halfway down the hair and get paler toward the tips. Balayage are streaks that are painted on.

Pop stars such as Katy Perry have set trends for blue, red, and pink hair.

The lighter red streaks in this model's hair have been painted on with a brush. This technique is called balayage.

FUTURE FACT

Hair colorings are very popular, and people are becoming more and more adventurous. Recently, celebrities have been adding gray to their hair! They bleach their hair silver white, or add silver or gray streaks or tips.

Covering up gray

Gray hair is associated with growing old, so it is not surprising that many people with gray hair want to change their hair color. Older women often add blonde streaks to their gray hair, but men usually dye their hair a darker color.

STRAIGHT OR CURLY?

Which Americans spend most on hair care? According to Treasured Locks, a company that sells hair-care products, African American women spend between double and six times what other Americans spend on hair care. One of the most common treatments they buy is hair relaxing, which softens and straightens the hair.

Hair relaxers

Hair relaxers use strong chemicals to soften and relax the hair. The strongest ones can easily damage the hair and scalp. Hair relaxing and straightening should only be done by an expert in a salon.

African American hair is naturally very curly. Strong chemicals must be used to relax the hair to make it straight.

The trend for brightly colored hair has led to an increase in demand for colored hair extensions.

Hair extensions

Why waste time growing your hair when you can buy hair extensions to attach to your own hair? That is what many women think, and the market in hair extensions is growing. Extensions make a lot of money for hair salons.

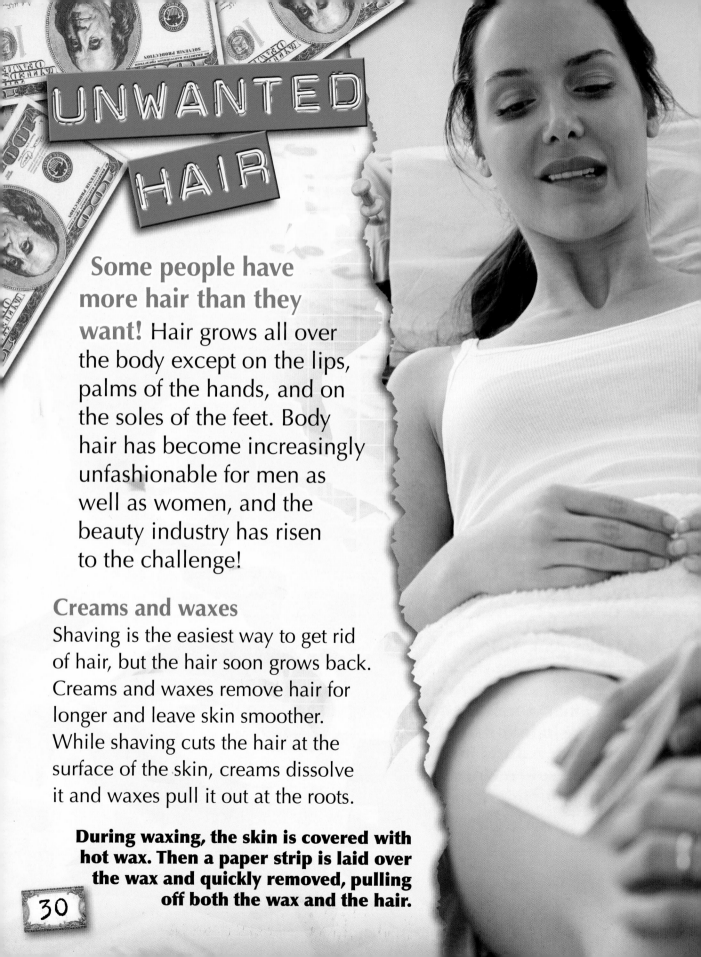

UNWANTED HAIR

Some people have more hair than they want! Hair grows all over the body except on the lips, palms of the hands, and on the soles of the feet. Body hair has become increasingly unfashionable for men as well as women, and the beauty industry has risen to the challenge!

Creams and waxes

Shaving is the easiest way to get rid of hair, but the hair soon grows back. Creams and waxes remove hair for longer and leave skin smoother. While shaving cuts the hair at the surface of the skin, creams dissolve it and waxes pull it out at the roots.

During waxing, the skin is covered with hot wax. Then a paper strip is laid over the wax and quickly removed, pulling off both the wax and the hair.

FUTURE FACT

Laser hair removal is expected to grow, making more money for salons and manufacturers. In 2010, sales of laser devices reached $1.1 billion worldwide, and by 2017, they are expected to reach $2.4 billion.

Laser hair removal

Electrolysis uses electricity to kill the hair root and so remove hairs one by one. Lasers, which use a beam of light to do much the same thing, are taking over this market, as larger areas can be treated more quickly.

SHAVING

When did shaving become big business? Sales of Gillette's safety razor with disposable blades boomed after every soldier fighting in the United States Army was supplied with one during World War I. Today, companies compete to produce better razors, blades, shaving creams, and shaving lotions.

Razor sharp

Electric razors were invented in 1928, but safety razors stayed popular. Many men prefer to use a traditional razor with water and shaving foam or gel. Companies selling shaving products to men often use the language of fast cars and jet planes for their products, such as Gillette's Mach 3 Turbo cartridge.

Most men shave every day. Shaving is big business for companies selling razors and shaving foam.

Shaving foams, creams, and lotions

Companies are constantly developing new or better shaving products, such as gels that irritate the skin less, preshaving lotions, and aftershaves. The biggest companies are those that produce razors, such as Gillette, and those that make other skin-care products.

Razors are made for women, too. Women use them to shave their legs and under their arms.

FUTURE FACT

Sales of shaving and hair-removal products are growing, but not very quickly. By 2012, they are expected to be 10 percent higher than they were in 2007. This is much less than laser hair removal (see page 31).

CHAPTER 4

UNDER THE KNIFE

Why is cosmetic surgery so expensive? Cosmetic surgery is done to change a person's looks, not to improve their health. This means that the operations are not necessary and so are not usually covered by health insurance. Cosmetic surgeons increase their earnings by charging the highest prices that they think patients will pay.

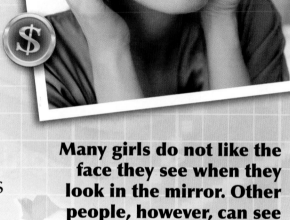

Many girls do not like the face they see when they look in the mirror. Other people, however, can see nothing wrong with it!

Common operations

The most popular operation is changing the size or shape of the breasts. This is done by implanting a silicone rubber shell filled with silicone gel or salt water. Liposuction is almost as popular. In this operation, fat is sucked out of selected areas, such as the thighs, hips, or tummy.

FIGHTING FAT

Only small amounts of fat can be removed by liposuction. It is not a solution for the growing problem of obesity. The only way to lose weight overall is to eat a healthy diet and exercise regularly.

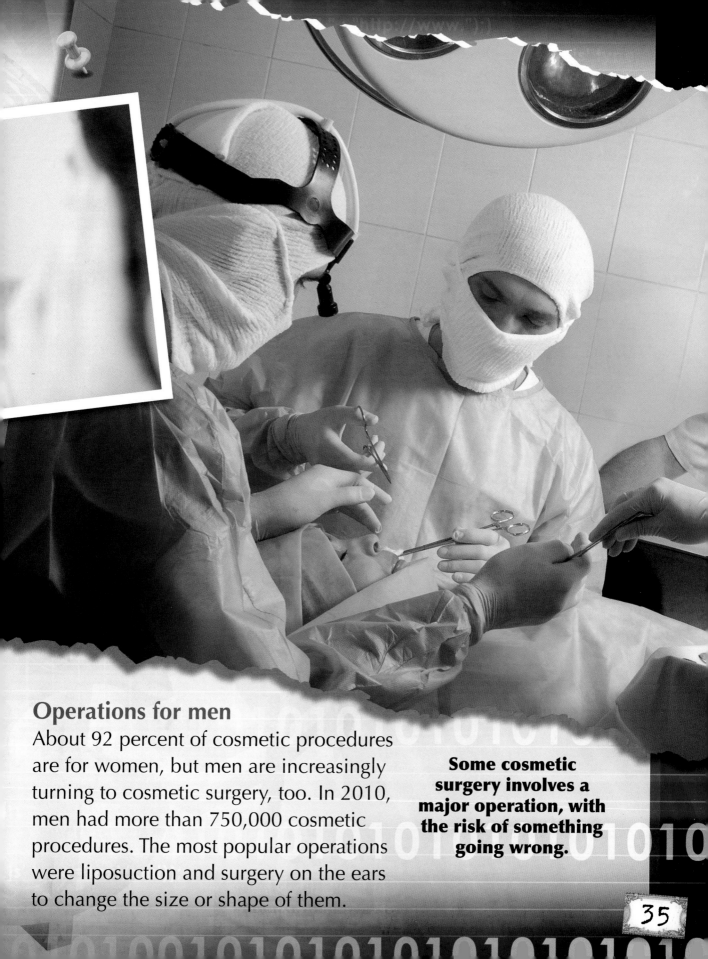

Operations for men

About 92 percent of cosmetic procedures are for women, but men are increasingly turning to cosmetic surgery, too. In 2010, men had more than 750,000 cosmetic procedures. The most popular operations were liposuction and surgery on the ears to change the size or shape of them.

Some cosmetic surgery involves a major operation, with the risk of something going wrong.

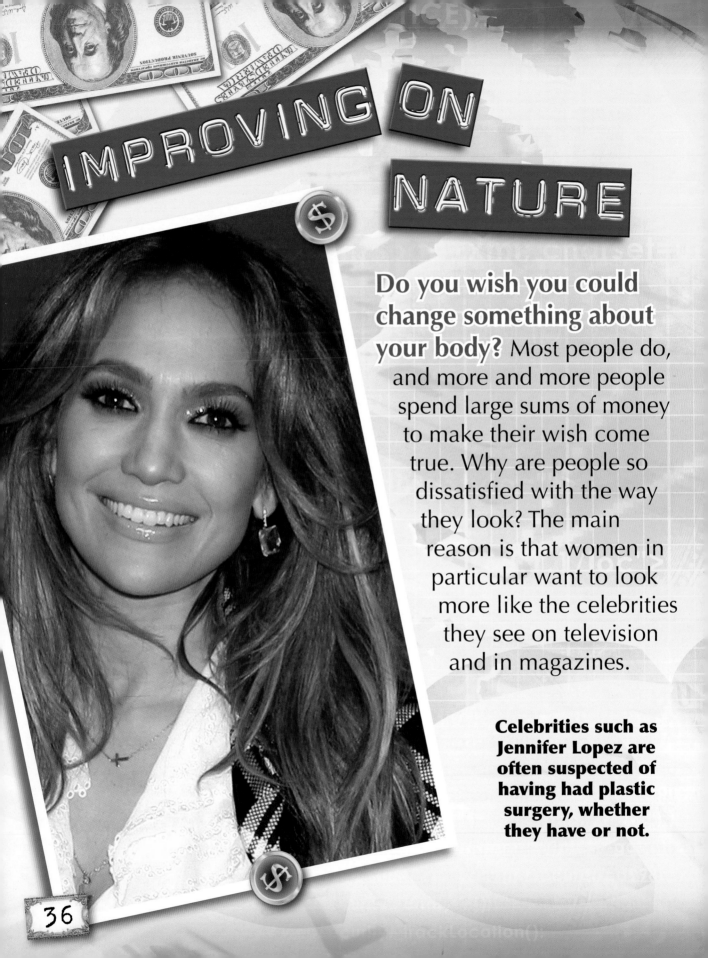

IMPROVING ON NATURE

Do you wish you could change something about your body? Most people do, and more and more people spend large sums of money to make their wish come true. Why are people so dissatisfied with the way they look? The main reason is that women in particular want to look more like the celebrities they see on television and in magazines.

Celebrities such as Jennifer Lopez are often suspected of having had plastic surgery, whether they have or not.

Media images

Models and movie stars rely on their looks to earn their living. They spend a lot of time and money to look the way they do. Cosmetic surgery is the most expensive and extreme way of changing a person's appearance.

Most women would love to have a slim waistline like this model. Some even have liposuction to get it!

FUTURE FACT

Business analysts have predicted that by 2012, up to 16 million Americans will be spending an incredible $2.5 billion a year on cosmetic surgery.

Young and slim

Models are almost always young and extremely slim. Many women feel a failure if they do not match up to the impossible standard of celebrities. Youthful looks are the most admired, which means that most older women try to look younger than they are.

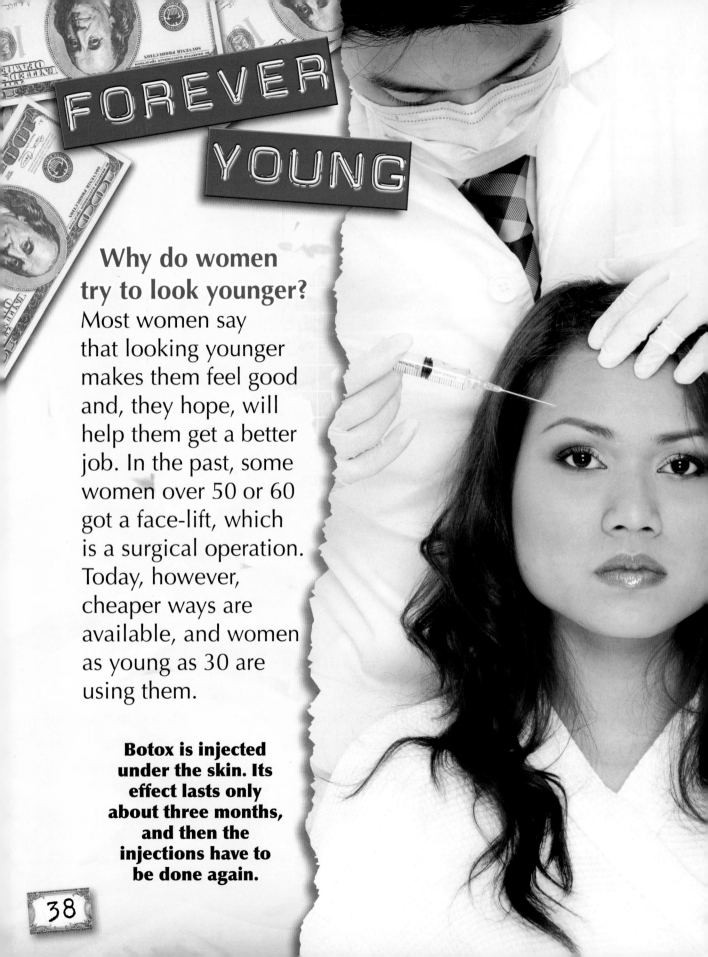

FOREVER YOUNG

Why do women try to look younger? Most women say that looking younger makes them feel good and, they hope, will help them get a better job. In the past, some women over 50 or 60 got a face-lift, which is a surgical operation. Today, however, cheaper ways are available, and women as young as 30 are using them.

Botox is injected under the skin. Its effect lasts only about three months, and then the injections have to be done again.

38

Botox bonanza

The most popular cosmetic procedure is an injection of botulinum toxin, or Botox. In large quantities, this is a dangerous poison, but a small amount injected into a muscle makes the muscle relax. It is mainly used to get rid of fine wrinkles.

Even young women are using antiaging creams in the hope that they will prevent wrinkles and other signs of aging.

Antiaging creams

Creams that reduce wrinkles and make skin look younger are big business. Different creams are sold for use around the eyes and lips, as well as for the whole face. Companies charge more for antiaging creams than for regular cosmetics, and the market is likely to increase.

TOO MUCH BOTOX

Cosmetic surgeons in the United States and the United Kingdom have reported that some women become hooked on Botox. When too much is used, or it is used too often, the woman's face looks frozen, and she cannot smile properly.

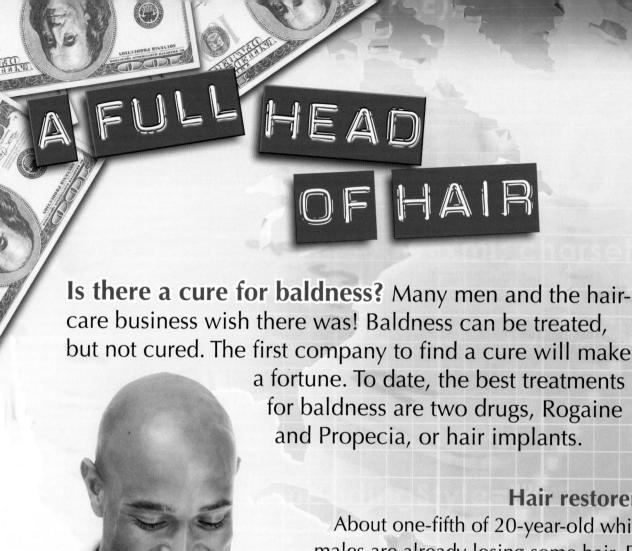

A FULL HEAD OF HAIR

Is there a cure for baldness? Many men and the hair-care business wish there was! Baldness can be treated, but not cured. The first company to find a cure will make a fortune. To date, the best treatments for baldness are two drugs, Rogaine and Propecia, or hair implants.

Hair restorers

About one-fifth of 20-year-old white males are already losing some hair. By the age of 50, about half of white men are beginning to go bald. Rogaine and Propecia contain a drug that slows the process down and encourages new hair to grow. As soon as the man stops the drug, however, the baldness simply returns.

Many men are happy being bald. Some even choose it by shaving their heads.

40

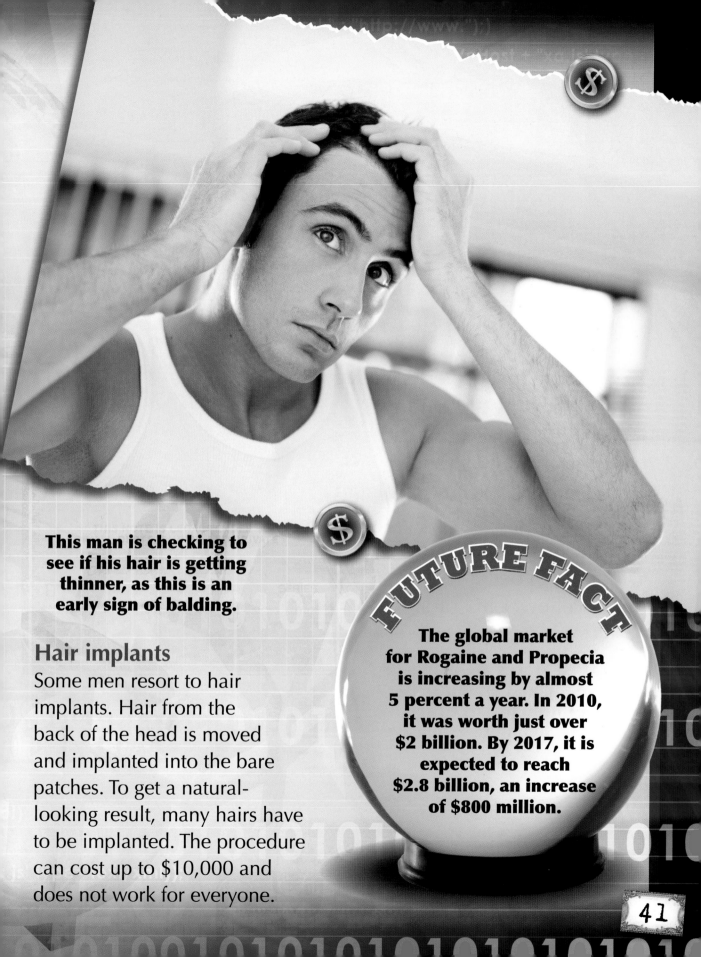

This man is checking to see if his hair is getting thinner, as this is an early sign of balding.

Hair implants

Some men resort to hair implants. Hair from the back of the head is moved and implanted into the bare patches. To get a natural-looking result, many hairs have to be implanted. The procedure can cost up to $10,000 and does not work for everyone.

FUTURE FACT

The global market for Rogaine and Propecia is increasing by almost 5 percent a year. In 2010, it was worth just over $2 billion. By 2017, it is expected to reach $2.8 billion, an increase of $800 million.

THE PERFECT SMILE

Even and straight

Straight teeth not only improve a person's smile but also are easier to clean, and this helps to keep the teeth and gums healthy. Some braces are designed to change the position of the lower jaw, so that the person's "bite" works better.

Do perfect teeth make a perfect smile? Cosmetic dentists have persuaded most of us that the answer is yes. Improving the appearance and color of teeth is big business. Many children (and some adults) have braces fitted to straighten crooked teeth. As people get older, their teeth become worn and yellower in color.

Most braces are made of metal. Ceramic or see-through braces are invisible, but more expensive.

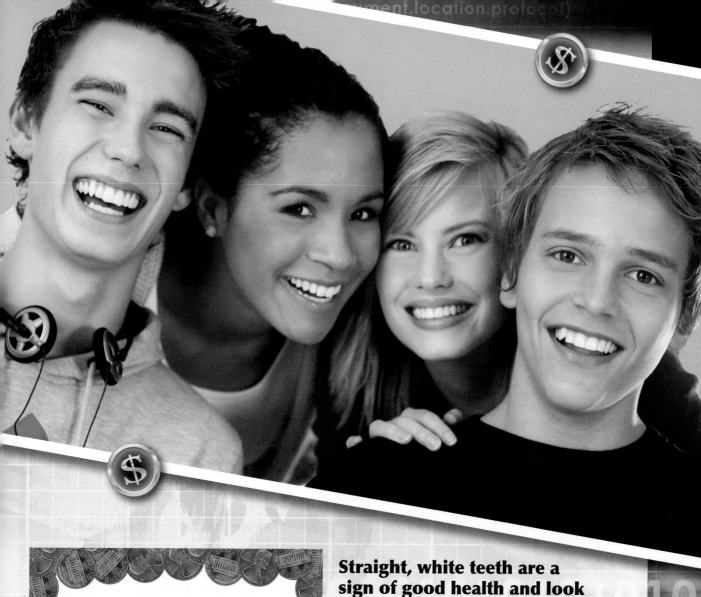

BUYING OVERSEAS

Some cosmetic dentistry is so expensive that many Americans go abroad for treatment. Prices in India, Singapore, and the United Kingdom, for example, are cheaper. If a problem arises after the treatment, however, it can be difficult to get it fixed.

Straight, white teeth are a sign of good health and look attractive when people smile.

Whiter and brighter

Toothpaste that contains whitener is cheap, but it can only do so much. Veneers and lumineers are special surfaces that are fixed over the teeth. They cost up to $2,000 a tooth. Even more expensive are tooth implants, which are fixed into the jawbone.

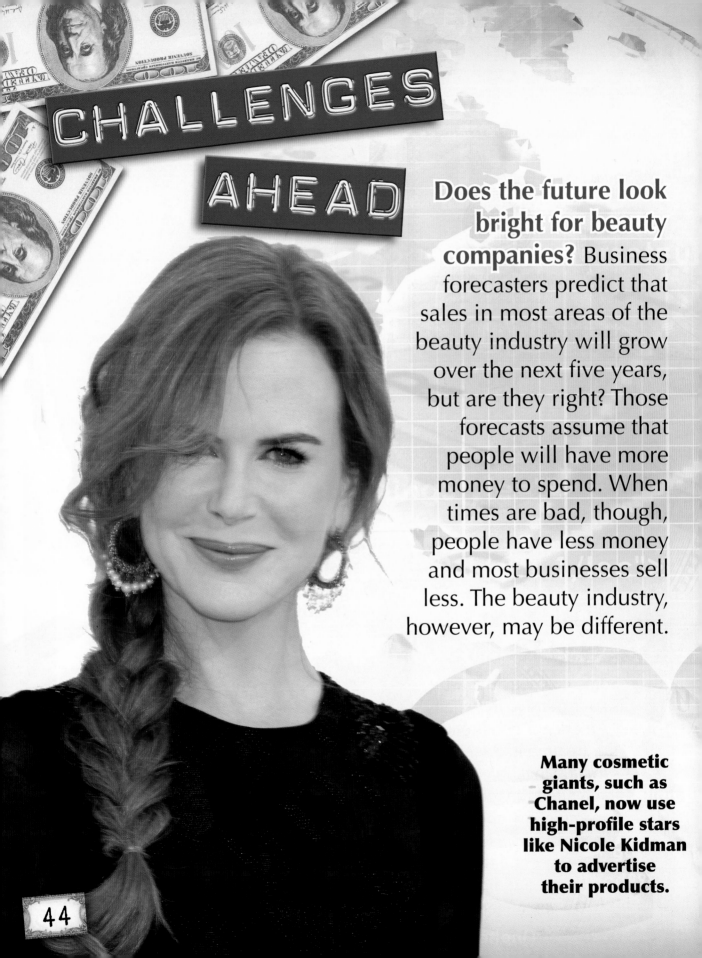

CHALLENGES AHEAD

Does the future look bright for beauty companies? Business forecasters predict that sales in most areas of the beauty industry will grow over the next five years, but are they right? Those forecasts assume that people will have more money to spend. When times are bad, though, people have less money and most businesses sell less. The beauty industry, however, may be different.

Many cosmetic giants, such as Chanel, now use high-profile stars like Nicole Kidman to advertise their products.

Appearance matters

When businesses are doing badly, people become worried about losing their job or about finding a job at all. Instead of spending less on cosmetics, many people spend more. They want to look their best to impress employers and secure a job.

Celebrity beauty products are a growing trend. Many stars, such as Halle Berry, are launching their own cosmetics.

FUTURE FACT

Looking and feeling beautiful has been linked to good health. The beauty industry has responded quickly to this by producing more natural and organic brands of cosmetics and hair care. What else may follow?

New trends and products

The beauty industry continues to develop new and better products. Clinique makes cosmetics for people with sensitive skins, who may suffer from allergies. It charges high prices for its products and is said to be Estée Lauder's most successful brand.

GLOSSARY

animal testing testing a product on an animal. Companies can only use ingredients that have been tested on animals or people, but the tests often cause the animals to suffer.

aromatherapy a treatment based on the external use of aromatic plant oils to maintain and promote good health

beautician a person who has trained to give beauty treatments, such as applying makeup and manicures

beauty products creams, lotions, makeup, and nail and hair products that people use to improve and take care of their appearance

cartridge a container that holds goods, such as a set of razors

cosmetics products that people use to care for their skin or hair and to make themselves look better

cosmetic surgery operation performed, or injections taken, to improve the way a person looks

economist a person who studies how goods, services, and wealth are produced, sold, and bought

electrolysis a way of removing hair roots by using an electric current

face-lift cosmetic surgery which lifts the skin on the face to remove wrinkles and sagging flesh

facial beauty treatment for the face that may include massage, cleansing the skin, and makeup

hair relaxer a lotion or cream that contains strong chemicals that make curly hair straighter and softer

highlighter a product that picks out particular parts of the hair, or the face

implant something that is inserted into parts of the body using surgery

kohl black powder that contains some metals. It is traditionally used as eyeliner, applied with a kohl pencil.

laser a strong, narrow beam of light

manicurist a person who trims, cleans, and polishes someone else's nails

massage rubbing the skin and muscles

meditation a form of relaxation that calms and focuses the mind

moisturizing making something, such as skin, less dry by applying creams

natural ingredients ingredients that come from plants or animals

radiation energy in the form of rays

research actions taken to find out new information about a particular subject

safety razor a razor in which the blade is mostly covered so that a person is less likely to cut themselves by mistake

silicone a type of synthetic material that feels like rubber

skin care cosmetics or actions for taking care of the skin

spa a luxurious hotel or other place where different types of beauty treatments, such as massages and facials, are available

specialized to do with a particular subject

sunscreen cream or lotion that protects skin from being damaged by the sun's rays

FOR MORE INFORMATION

BOOKS

Bochner, Arthur, and Rose Bochner. *The New Totally Awesome Business Book for Kids*. New York, NY: Newmarket Press, 2007.

Crump, Marguerite. *No B.O.! The Head-to-Toe Book of Hygiene for Preteens*. Minneapolis, MN: Free Spirit Publishing, 2005.

Smith, Allison Chandler. *The Girls' World Book of Bath and Beauty*. New York, NY: Lark Books, 2004.

WEBSITES

Find out more about the beauty industry at:

www.chemistscorner.com/how-to-become-a-cosmetic-chemist

www.cosmeticsinfo.org/history3.php

www.treasuredlocks.com/black-hair-care-industry.html

Publisher's note to educators and parents: Our editors have carefully reviewed these websites to ensure that they are suitable for students. Many websites change frequently, however, and we cannot guarantee that a site's future contents will continue to meet our high standards of quality and educational value. Be advised that students should be closely supervised whenever they access the Internet.

INDEX